My Traumas and Me

A Memoir

My Traumas and Me

A Memoir

CATHERINE BROWN

This book is dedicated to all the people who have supported me and to all the survivors out there who struggle every day to keep going.

'Keep riding the train in the darkness... the light will come'

CONTENTS

1. INTO THE DARK WITH NO WAY OUT

Whenever something truly bad happens, there's always a trigger point you can track back to where the situation might have been averted. Something you could have done – or in my case, *not* done – that could have averted danger.

This time, it was a simple text.

I was a 19-year-old city girl who had just been promoted to a supervisor at work. I had put in a 13-hour shift at the petrol station and faced the same again the next day. I needed an early night. My partner, who wasn't in work, had invited some friends over.

'I'll just head on upstairs now,' I had said to everyone round about 10 p.m.

Two, three hours later the music from below pounded on.

Boom! Boom! I was desperate to sleep, but couldn't.

I composed my text with care.

'Amy, please can you turn the music down,' I keyed in. 'I have an early start for work tomorrow.'

Within moments I heard heavy boots on the stairs. Then, those same boots kicked open our bedroom door.

'How dare you be disrespectful to me when I am having a party downstairs!' shouted my partner Amy. 'You are a total waste of space!'

With that, and her true opinion of me blasted out, my girlfriend of six months or so turned to leave the room.

'I can't do this anymore,' I replied to her back. 'I am done.'

In my mind, I imagined what life might be like without a girlfriend whose sudden mood swings meant she could be cuddled up to me one moment, sharing and showing how much she loved me, but then spitting onto my face – literally spitting – the next.

Each morning, when I woke up beside her in the rundown housing association house I had worked hard to keep spotless, I never knew which Amy I would find. The place was in her name and several months ago, I had secretly packed a bag of clothing basics and hidden it in a closet in the bathroom. I had wanted to be ready to leave if ever her casual violence of flicking the side of my head with her thumb and forefinger or slapping my cheek escalated further.

Perhaps now was that time? I was loyal and loving and tried to be the partner she wanted. But didn't I deserve something back in return?

I got out of bed and walked towards the hall.

Amy was quicker. As I went to leave the room, she turned back towards me, grabbed me under the arms and threw me back onto our bed. I was aware of her weight pinning me down, and I remember feeling momentarily relieved that she hadn't straightened out the fingers of her right hand, which would have meant she could have been about to deliver a slap. But then I saw why – and it was much worse.

That hand was holding a knife.

As it came nearer to my face, I took in the white handle and how the pointed blade was around three inches or so. It was an old man's flick-out razor blade; the sort you might see in old movies, when the hero is getting a shave at a barbershop. I had no idea at all how Amy came to have one; nor why she would want to get it out now. I was hot with fear, so perhaps that was why the blade felt particularly cold as she ran it very lightly along my neck. Thank God I wasn't shaking too.

'I want to slit your throat,' she said. Those exact words.

I bit my lip, all the more to keep my body, and more essentially my throat, totally still.

She lifted the blade from my neck and begin to circle it, high above my face.

'Look up Kat. Look up.'

I didn't know what she meant me to do, but I was desperate not to get it wrong. I could smell alcopop on her breath.

'The bulb, you moron,' she continued, pointing now at the ceiling light. 'One of these days I am going to hang you from that.'

If my face showed even half the terror I felt, then that must have been enough for her. She had got her 'kick' out of seeing me utterly under her control. She backed away.

'Everything OK in there?'

That was her cousin's voice from the hall – and my opportunity for escape.

'Paul! Help!' I cried out, getting off the bed, but finding that my legs gave way. I dropped down onto my knees, then carried on speaking.

'She pulled a knife on me,' I stuttered, still too shocked to say more to Paul, who was by now in the bedroom too.

'Ah, she's talking shit,' said Amy. 'Do you honestly believe that I would do that? I love her!'

I could see from his face that this cousin was ready to believe Amy, not me. He looked at me with contempt, as if I were something you would wipe from your shoe.

I was not surprised. All my life, people have not believed me. Yet I find it impossible to tell lies. Even as a small child, I would own up to taking a pound coin that fell on the floor when my father drunkenly stumbled in from the pub. Or I would be the one that smiled then changed the subject if my sister asked if she looked OK when wearing a shabby, hand-me-down dress. I say the truth, or keep silent with it. I am no better than anyone else for doing this, it is just how I am. I am honest, but I hate upsetting people.

I also learnt early on that, given the choice between the truth and keeping silent, keeping silent may be the easier option. Even when the subject matter is just about the most terrible things one person can do to another, the consequences of exposing those terrible things can be even worse than letting them continue.

That night, with Amy and Paul, my mind raced back to the very worst example.

A few days before my 13th birthday, I gathered my family together to confront them with the revolting and shocking truth that TWO family members had been sexually abusing me. The devastating result was not one that anyone might expect.

'You've got it wrong Kat,' I was told. 'We don't believe you.'

'You're a liar,' said the man who had subjected me to six years of escalating abuse, then rape. 'I would never have touched you.'

'We have only your word for it,' said a police officer. 'Without anyone else backing you, it's not enough.'

'We can't get involved,' said my church group. 'If we are asked, we are going to deny that you told us about it. You are on your own with this.'

Then the final blow from my own mother: 'If anything did happen, it was your fault.'

So was it my fault now that Amy had drawn a knife on me, because I had said out loud, 'I can't do this anymore' when I could have kept that desperation to myself?

Amy must have flicked the blade down, because the white of the handle glinted under the brightness of the light.

'What the fuck,' said Paul. But Amy had no intention of answering. She ran past him, then downstairs and out the house and onto the street.

This was my moment to leave. So I too ran out the front door. We lived in the city centre, so my plan was to get the night bus out of here – to anywhere really. A hostel. An all-night burger place. I hadn't thought it through.

I had walked for perhaps five minutes when she appeared, suddenly, from an alleyway. She stepped right onto my path, so we were on the street together, less than two yards apart. Illuminated by a street light, I gasped as once again my eyes went straight to the knife.

She was holding the blade up against her bare, outstretched arm.

'You are not leaving me,' she said. 'If you don't come back, I will kill myself.'

Already, she was ripping up her arm with the blade. The pressure was light, so the red that appeared was in streaks, not gushes. Like ripples through an ice-cream rather than deep, damaging cuts.

'I don't care,' I said. 'You kill yourself then.'

But both she and I knew that this wouldn't be how it played out.

'Your behaviour to me is awful,' I cried.

I was close enough to snatch the knife away from her now. But I didn't want any sudden movement from me to cause her to plunge the blade more deeply and dangerously into her arm. I had to take a 'softly, softly' approach.

'What do you want from me?' I asked.

'You are coming back with me,' she said and we both knew that it was no longer a question. I turned around and went back into the house with her.

The woman who was abusing me had won again, only now I was more trapped than ever.

That night, I believed that there was no way out. I could not put my own suffering above the possibility that Amy might have killed herself. Every reasonable person would, I believe, have acted the same.

By the time we got back to the house, everyone else had left.

'I'll get help. I know I need it,' my girlfriend told me as we sat on the sofa. 'I will see someone tomorrow.'

I am not aware that she ever saw anyone.

Instead, many years later, it would be me who went on to see people. Psychiatrists. Psychologists. My GP. By the very fact that I am writing this book, you will have worked out that I did find the courage to break free from Amy. But I went on to endure other abusive relationships too.

It is only now, age 33 and engaged to marry the love of my life, that I feel able to write down my story. It is a brutal, shocking tale of abuse. I make no excuse for that, because the purpose of sharing what happened to me is too important. I want to help others find the courage to break free sooner than I did, and I want to put it out loud and clear that child sexual abuse can never be that child's 'fault.'

At one point, I actively tried to end my life; at many, many others I existed rather than lived. Professionals who have helped me say that the seeds of what happened were sewn during my earliest years. They use the term 'neglect.' I tend to be more forgiving and generous, because I believe my parents in particular did the best that they could do, given circumstances which you will read about. Currently I see them several times a week.

It is for you the reader to decide what you feel about my family. I am writing this anonymously, because even after all that has happened, I don't wish for them to be recognised by their friends or neighbours, which might go on to upset them. Also, I remain in fear of one of my attackers. I have received threats that my house will be burnt out; I have also been told I will be killed. Names in their story have been changed as have some specific, identifying details.

There is no ambiguity however, on **why** I am telling my story. Like most victims of child abuse and domestic violence, I survived by turning in on myself. I hated what was happening but believed I had no control to stop it. I had no voice. I became invisible.

Now and with this book, I do have a voice. If you have experienced or are experiencing abuse, I need to tell you that you can break free. It is hard, but if you keep on going, you can do it. There is light at the end of the tunnel.

Writing my book has taken me back to very dark places. It may be that you find some passages upsetting. Please know that everything I have shared is with the hope that it may help others.

I have chosen to begin my story as it continued – with explosive, high drama. When I was three years old, I was left unsupervised with a box of matches. This would be the first of several house fires that would leave their mark on me, each in different ways.

But I'm getting ahead of myself. I'll continue my story right at the beginning of a young life that really should have been lived in a very different way.

2. TRAPPED IN A PARTY HOUSE

There's something mesmerising about fire. One minute, you're striking a small stick against a tiny, rough-edged box, the next a dark room is flooded with light. This was how it seemed to me, aged around three, and a little lad from down the street who often popped round. We didn't understand about danger and how fast things can get out of hand.

It was early evening, and we had been up in the tiny bedroom I shared with my middle sister. Then Dad had come upstairs, drunk, and laid on my sister's bed. He and Mum had been kipping on the couch downstairs whilst they decorated their room, and he had stumbled into where we were, and taken over. He had emptied his pockets before he had fallen into sleep, casually pulling out coins, matches and cigarettes onto the blanket. Within moments, there was rough snoring. Time for us to find somewhere else to play!

I picked up the matches, with no real thought about it, and headed for my parents' bedroom. We didn't mind that it was cluttered with pots of paint, white spirit and decorating cloths. We shut the door and then sat on the floor.

For something to do, I began striking the matches. It was fun in a very young child way to watch the flame burst from nowhere, then die away as the match stick withered. But then one match didn't wither.

Perhaps it dropped onto a piece of cloth that had highly flammable white spirit on it. We were too young to know anything about how chemicals work. Within moments, a huge well of flame began licking up the wall opposite. Too transfixed to move, I reached over to the bed to grab at a red blanket, and pulled it over our heads. Even through the blanket, the room glowed. The air changed too. It smelt and sounded like the 11th July celebrations that were common across Northern Ireland. All smoke and dust and crackles.

'Help!' I screamed, loud as I could us. 'Won't you help us?!'

And then my memory of that dreadful evening stops.

Mum has told me that, from the galley kitchen downstairs, she heard my screams but that she couldn't get up the narrow stairs to rescue me, because the smoke was so intense. I do know, because I have been told, that I was carried downstairs by a fire and rescue officer. Thankfully, no one was injured. The biggest repercussion was how neighbours viewed me afterwards.

I would be taunted in the streets.

'You're a firesetter,' I was told. 'You're not safe to be around.'

No one pointed any blame at my father, for leaving matches unattended.

I think no one challenged my father because, to the outside world Dad was a lovely, friendly guy who made pals quickly. No one would perhaps believe that he was also so casual and careless around his children, when he clearly loved them a good deal. One of 13 himself, many of dad's enormous family lived in the terraced streets around us, and liked to party just

MY TRAUMAS AND ME

as much as Dad. Beer tended to be OK, but when he had cider inside him, he was a different man. He would change from friendly to shouty in a sentence. And when on the rare occasions he had spirits inside him, then he was a nasty, nasty man…

Yet it's important to me to be fair to both my Dad and Mum. So I need to share a little of their back stories, before I arrived into the world in 1989.

There are good reasons why they were like they were. Dad's childhood had been tough: can you imagine 13 children shoe-boxed into a two-bedroom terraced house?! When his mother died at 52 from heart disease, he was still a boy. He signed up to the army for a change of scene. He had left to do casual labouring and gardening work by the time he met mum when he was 24.

Now and again, my parents would enjoy telling the story of how they got together. They had both gone to sit on the same large chair in a pub, when it tipped over – and Dad fell into a fridge-freezer. I don't know why there was a fridge-freezer in a corner of a pub. But it certainly broke the ice. They started going out together from that night!

Like Dad, Mum's childhood hadn't been easy. Except for a set of twins, each of her four brothers and sisters had a different father. By the time she met Dad, Mum already had an 'out of wedlock' child too – my sister Ellie, who is 12 years older than me.

Granny swore by this amazing story that Mum's dad (and my grandfather) had been a six foot-plus sailor in the merchant navy who went back to Canada, even before their child arrived. Years later, when I gave mum a DNA kit as a Christmas present, her ancestry was revealed to be 100% Irish/Scottish/English. So I think Granny may have been spinning a tall tale.

My paternal Granddad was a caring man. Once Mum became pregnant with my middle sister, he gave Dad no room for manoeuvre.

'You've got her into trouble. Now you must marry,' he declared. Granny (that's mum's mother) helped my parents apply for a housing association house and said that she would keep Ellie with her, to give my parents the very best chance of their relationship working out. Little Ellie flitted between both houses.

Even from the start, though, the cracks in my parents' marriage were there. Dad had strident views he insisted on enforcing. Mum, who is petite and less than five foot tall, liked to keep up with fashion and make-up trends. One day, Dad decided this needed to stop. He took her over to the kitchen sink, then scrubbed off her make-up so hard that she never wore cosmetics again. Over time, she also took less interest in clothes and her appearance generally. She became watchful and wary.

'Never irritate your father,' she would tell us. 'When he gets home, don't make too much noise.'

Whilst loving in his language and actions towards me, Dad was rough and rude to Mum.

'You slut,' he would shout out at her, if she had dressed in a way that he didn't feel was appropriate. 'You whore,' he would blast out when he wanted to close down an argument.

It always worked. Mum never felt able to shake off the 'shame' of having been a single mum. When he taunted her, she backed down.

I never saw my father hit my mother. But verbal abuse also packs a strong psychological punch. Mum became (and remains) broken. As a young woman, Mum had worked in a shirt factory. But through all the years of my growing up, Mum never went to work again, staying largely at home and in the shadows.

Now and again, with a martini inside her, she'd shout back at Dad. Then they would each give as good as they got, perhaps for hours. I remember sitting on the stairs, hugging my sister tight. Both of us willed for the rows to stop. They seldom did.

As with many unhappy families, we had been through real tragedy – but no one had been able to process or express difficult feelings, so they had turned into shouting and anger. In our case, those difficult feelings were about grief.

Whilst my middle sister and I arrived into the world totally healthy babies, Mum also had two more children that died either at or shortly after birth.

One of these babies was born before me and the other was around three years after me. I have few details, only fragments of memory. I can picture a sister lying in an open coffin in our house, as we waited for the funeral hearse. I wonder now if my other sister was stillborn – because for years in our house the only pictures of her were taken posthumously. They hung on the living room wall, put there by Dad, as a memorial. On two days each year, we would commemorate my lost sisters' birthdays. I was told that one sister was buried in hospital grounds, and I never knew where the other one was. It was all achingly sad.

When I was around four, one of my father's brothers would go on to trash our house. As he threw a microwave through the living room window and swung his fists and furnishings around, the pictures of my dead sisters would be destroyed. There were other copies.

This particular fall-out had been sparked by one of Dad's brothers and a cousin both seeing the same woman. Dad had stepped in to calm the peace, but it hadn't worked. Dad and his brothers and cousins frequently fought, with or without cause. When naturally volatile people are 'in drink,' a word wrongly taken can quickly escalate to a punch-up.

No one truly fell out with anyone though; quarrels were forgotten as night after night our house remained the party house. Our extensive family, their partners and friends, came over to share beers, swap stories – and have the occasional fight. The smoke from everyone's cigarettes and the thump of country music filled my childhood bedroom. Even with my big sister for comfort, I couldn't settle to sleep.

Now and again, Dad went to prison; he would simply say he been a 'bad boy.' I think it may have been for unpaid fines. Dad was no hardened criminal, but he did sail close to the wind. He would keep things at our house, 'for a mate.' Once, I remember there was so much pine disinfectant being stored, we could hardly get to the bathroom!

There was never enough money coming in and Mum talked about how Dad spent our child benefit money on drink;

therefore she always had cash loans, taken out from a man who called at the door. Right through my childhood we would hide behind the sofa when the doorbell went, because she didn't have the money for that week's repayment.

Dad visited the loans man too. Every Christmas, we would have new shoes or trainers that he paid for this way.

My parents loved us, I know that with certainty. It's just that their lives were chaotic. When Dad daytime-drank in the street with other men, he would take me along too. Sometimes Mum would rock up.

'If you can't beat them, Kat, then join them,' she would say.

Dad and his mates called themselves 'The Wine Team.' I would spend hours cooped up in my buggy whilst the adults sat on brick walls and necked beers. Now and again, men leaned in or spoke over my pram, bringing with them a pungent mix of aftershave and alcohol. I hate both smells to this day.

Sometimes, my sister and I would effectively be home alone, as my parents were upstairs and asleep. Once, an aunt arrived to find us crying. I was in a dirty nappy and my sister had her finger stuck inside an empty can of Carlsberg. Many was the time she would scoop us up and take us back to her own home or to Granny's. At other times, my big sister would step in. She provided the hugs that Mum didn't like to do. She took the time to get the nits from my hair. She would cuddle me close and say, 'It's going to be alright Kat,' even though we both knew that it would not.

Social services were never quite on the case. I don't know who tipped them off, but Mum always seemed to get wind of when someone from the council was due. She would tidy the house and her daughters.

'Nothing to see here,' she would tell social workers.

Once, I had been playing in the street when a brick fragment got thrown at my head. I ran into the house, gushing blood, and Mum's response was to get a tea towel. When the dad of the little lad who had thrown the brick came into our house, he told Mum she needed to take me into A&E for stitches. She did not. She didn't want any attention from the authorities, regardless of what happened.

Mum's parenting style was that we had a bath on Sunday to be clean for the week. I was aged around 10 when I discovered that good hygiene takes much more.

'So how often should we brush our teeth?' a dentist asked my class.

'Once a week,' I replied confidently. 'Unless you're an adult that smokes, then it's twice daily.'

How my cheeks burned when I discovered the correct regime. That evening, I insisted Mum bought me own toothbrush and paste. It felt good to be in charge of something.

3. CHIP FIRES AND STREET FIGHTS

The fighting. The drinking. The partying. These are the abiding memories of my first years, and like all my early life, they happened within a few streets. Although the 'Troubles' were at full pelt in 1990s Northern Ireland, I wasn't anxious about the car bombings, street riots and sectarian murders that went on through the country. I had too much trauma going on in my own small world.

When a member of our family was imprisoned for political activities, Dad told me not to worry, because he would never be involved in anything like that, and I believed him. I believed in God too, but I didn't have an interest in religious politics. I am Protestant, and I was fine to mix with both Catholic and Protestant.

The taunts about my setting our house alight died down after a few months. But fire came to our house, again and again, mostly due to Dad. He had a habit of unwittingly putting on the chip pan on for some snacking, then falling asleep, leaving the pan on the stove. I can remember the soot on our small, frightened faces and being unable to see anyone as smoke filled the tiny galley kitchen. Mum would always dash in and smother the flames on the chip pan just in time.

It was totally his fault, but no one called Dad a firesetter. No one would dare.

After one fire that got more out of hand, we were rehoused. Another time we were rehoused to keep us safe from violent neighbours. Or was it our family that was moved, because neighbours had fallen out with us? Once we moved so fast that the house we went into had no carpet or furniture, or even any beds. We slept on a stone floor for a few nights until a charity provided second-hand items.

Of course, this 'casual violence' didn't only happen at our house. At a neighbour's, a lad pressed a 50 pence piece into my hand that he'd heated up in the oven. No one came to my rescue and there were no consequences for the boy, even though the burn on my hand was so severe that I have the scar to this day. It was a rough area and people just got on with what life threw their way.

Once, my paternal grandfather's house was set alight (everyone was out, thankfully). He had promised me that one day his old record player would belong to me. But it was destroyed. Plenty of other times my Granny's windows got smashed in.

I was six years old when I saw my father stabbed in the street. He was slashed three times in the stomach and chest by one of several guys who came out of a bush opposite our house.

It had been a typical night for my family. It was Halloween night and Dad and Mum were both drunk. Mum had bought me back to a neighbour's bedroom, where she had quickly fallen into a snoring sleep. I was at the window, watching Dad arguing with a man I didn't know. Two more guys appeared and then the knife must have been brought out. I didn't see the blade, but I saw the blood and heard Dad scream. He swung away, and his shoulder caught the knife. Next, Dad was on the ground screaming in pain.

Now I was screaming and screaming as well, but I couldn't rouse Mum. When I went back to the window, Dad was gone. This went on to become the stuff of my nightmares for years and years. In these nightmares, I could see the knife, and the blood, and Dad dropping to the ground, then vanishing.

Police were at the door in moments. It turned out that Dad had staggered to a house in the next street. In the ambulance that was blue-lighted to him, Dad's heart stopped beating and he needed to be resuscitated. 'I saw my dead mum in the ambulance,' he told me later. 'She said, "It's not your time yet son."'

The police spent the next day in our street. There was blood on our door and a bleeding trail into the bushes. But no one was caught. Dad has told me that he knew who did it, but he has never told me who that someone was.

My sister stayed with Granny, whilst Mum and I stayed with Mum's sister and her husband. We felt safer in a different part of town for a while. Dad joined us once he came out from hospital, and then it was arguments and drinking as usual. One night, dad fell asleep in the only bathroom. He had locked the door and we couldn't rouse him. We had to pee in a bucket.

Another time, there was so much shouting that someone called the police. From the top of the stairs, peeking through the slats, I watched two officers arrive. I remember hoping that now, someone was going to take me away from all this.

'I don't hit my wife,' Dad told the officers, and fetched Mum. 'You tell them,' he said to her. 'You tell them that there is nothing going on here.'

Ironically, Dad had been at school with one of the police officers. He bought what my father said. As the door closed, I remember thinking how Mum would be in trouble now.

To be honest, though, that was nothing compared to the horror that what was heading my way.

4. THE NEW BOYFRIEND

When your bed is positioned so that your feet are by the window, your head nearest to the door, you don't get to see who walks into the room. Instead, you hear the sounds and see the level of darkness change.

Back then, it was the creak of the door and the shaft of light from the hall creating a brightness along the length of my bed. Then I knew my ordeal was going to begin. I'd close my eyes tight and wait for the disgusting feel and taste that would follow.

This bed didn't have a frame, so my attacker could stand close behind my head. I would smell the aftershave on him as one hand rubbed my shoulders and the other moved on himself, just inches from my face. Next, I would clench my teeth as the result of his masturbating landed on my skin. Sometimes, he would wipe the fluid over my face.

Often, he would manage to prise apart my lips. I'd grind my teeth, willing none to land inside my mouth. Then he would disappear to return with a bathroom tissue and he would wipe my face. But there was nothing for my mouth. I would be left lying in bed tasting this horrible, slimy yukky stuff.

I didn't know what it was. There was no one I could ask.

I was seven years old.

I didn't understand anything sexual. But I did understand terror.

Each night that this happened, I was petrified. On the nights that it did not, I lay awake in fear that it might.

The total, dreadful irony of the situation was that this happened at a family member's house. It was a place where I was sent to stay when the situation at home was fraught. Mum and Dad, if they thought about it at all, would have think I was having a good time.

The family member, whose house it was, was kind and loving. She had no idea whatsoever of my ordeal. Why would she? My attacker was her daughter's new boyfriend. In company, he was OK. A bit nerdy about computer games, but otherwise quiet, respectful. He had a job. He appeared to enjoy dating a grown-up woman.

There were no outwards signs that he was a paedophile.

Or that, even as he went on to father a child, he was still, night after night, revealing and carrying out his true, perverted desires.

The abuse that was to last for six years had begun gradually. The whole family would be in the living room and he would start a game that involved chasing me. He would pull me onto the sofa and he would grasp me more tightly than other family members did. Or he would sit me on his knee, or bounce me on his lap.

Then, one day he came up to a bedroom where I was playing Nintendo. He sat beside me on the bed and stroked my shoulder. It felt odd, so I focused on *Mario All Stars* as he put his hand up the back of my shirt. I didn't know what to do; I was seven, he was 22. He moved his hand to the front, where my child's chest area was and continued to play with my skin.

'You know you are my favourite,' he said. 'Don't say anything to anybody.'

Was it was because I didn't that he took it further, bit by bit? It remains 100 per cent not my fault that this happened to me. But in dark moments, I do wonder if I had 'victim' written on my face. I had grown up being told not to upset or irritate anyone. To be good and invisible.

Daytime didn't provide an escape. Under the family dining table – even whilst everyone else was there too – this man would bring his hand under the table, then move it up my legs to press over my knickers. All the while, he would be chatting with the family, as if what he was doing wasn't happening.

This went on for some months. Then the night time ordeal began.

I always pretended to be asleep, but I am sure he realised I was not. He never spoke. Afterwards, in 'normal' times, he would tell me that if I told anyone, I would lose all my family. I would also ruin their lives, and specifically that of his girlfriend (who I was really close to). Later, once they had a child, he told me that I would be sent away and never see this baby (whom I had come to love greatly).

Once, he took me and his girlfriend and my middle sister on holiday. It was meant to be a huge treat, and it was generous. Aged nine, it was the first time I had stayed at the seaside. But it was blighted by this man. At one point, he saved my life in that when I was struggling in the swimming pool, he dived in to rescue me. But on the other hand, of course, he also ruined my life by what he did to me.

When my sister and I got sunburnt on that holiday, he was all eagerness to help. In the bath, he lotioned and rubbed the area between our legs again and again. He also touched himself as well as us. Today, my sister denies this happened, which I continue to find impossible to understand.

With a home of their own, plus a baby to keep my relative busy, the way was clear for my attacker to make even more vile demands of me. It was clear that he got a kick out of his 'secret' life.

Once, he walked down the stairs with his penis out, aware that from where we sat in the living room I would see this but his partner would not. Other times, when we were watching TV and my cousin would go into the kitchen to make a cuppa, he would fix his eyes on me and begin stroking his penis. If I got up to leave the room, he would drag me back onto the sofa and attempt to thrust his penis into me through my clothes.

It was shortly before I was 10 years old that the abuse escalated to sex. I was still too young to wear a bra. Up in the bedroom I always stayed in, he would lay me on the bed and pull up my top.

'You're going to turn out gorgeous,' he would tell me. 'You will know what to do, because I will have taught you.'

He would take my trousers and pants down and kiss down my belly. Then he would lie on top of me, and rub his penis into my vagina. He would try to put it inside me, and I cried a lot at this, because I was sore. My tears had no effect. He would come, just outside of my body, and then slide his fingers inside me to rub all the yukky stuff into me.

Afterwards, he would slope away and I would find myself in the bathroom, trying to clean myself up. Awful, awful, awful.

Another time, when my relative popped out, he grabbed me by the back of the neck and pushed me into the upstairs bathroom. He took his trousers down, sat on the toilet and made me put his penis in my mouth. Then he put his hand on the back of his head, forcing movement. I was choking and gagging. I wanted to shout out 'stop' but I couldn't even speak.

He was just getting himself sorted afterwards when the front door opened.

'Where's Kat?' came the call up from the hall. Next, high-heel boots thumped up the stairs, reaching the top just as he had walked away from the bathroom.

As soon as I dared, I came out and I gave my relative a pleading look. I wanted everything to stop – oh how I wanted it! But I didn't want to lose all my family. She looked straight back at me and, for one beautiful second, I thought, 'She knows. She is going to stop this for me.'

But then she began talking about something else and the moment was gone. Years later, she would say she didn't remember anything about my being in the bathroom when she got home. She most certainly had not known what was happening, she said.

I began my periods at 11. My attacker switched to attempting anal penetration. I understood more about sex now through lessons at school. I was disgusted as well as terrified. Knowing why what he was doing was illegal and wrong made me believe all the more that I had to keep my mouth shut. If I told anyone, then I truly would break up the family.

I loved my family. I was the type of child that did everything I could to please those around me. I could not do anything that might cause them pain and separation. Far better to suffer myself, alone.

5. BEHIND LOCKED DOORS

Every Friday, our family descended on a family member's house. Chip shop chips in gravy. Plenty of chit chat. And Mum finding confidence and beer-courage to shout back at Dad, because there were other family adults about.

'You don't want to be hearing that,' said the family member whose house it was. 'Why not pop up to Mike's room?'

Mike (not his real name), had never married. He was close to 30, had a job cleaning and liked to watch TV in his room. Mike had always been kind to me. If he found, say, a toy or a bracelet or a ring whilst he was cleaning out a former tenants home or car… he'd slip it into his overall, then give it to me. We also played cards together, which I enjoyed. I never felt threatened by him and, to be honest, it felt like a spot of relief from the terrible ordeal that was going on at my cousin's house. Up in his room, we would sit cosily on the top of his made-up single bed and watch *Coronation Street* and *EastEnders*. Sometimes my sister would come up too.

Then one Friday, when I was about 11, everything changed. I'd been sent me upstairs as my parents began to kick off. Only instead of just saying, 'Good to see you,' Mike got up from the bed and locked the bedroom door. Then when I sat down, he sat down really close to me.

In the time it takes for a man's hand to move off your shoulder and down onto your breast, our relationship went from being cosy uncle and niece to sex abuser and victim.

Mike had been drinking bottles of WKD.

'Do you want one?' he asked. I said no and shrugged his hand from my breast. Instead of letting me go, he put that arm back across the front of my neck, so tightly I felt I was choking. Then, he dropped his other hand onto my leg and moved it along so that it was pushing against my vagina.

'Get off me! Get off me,' I shouted and his grip slackened.

I bolted to the door, undid the lock and ran downstairs.

I didn't know what to do.

'Is the taxi coming to take us home?' I asked Mum. This was always how we went back. She said I could ring for it, and I sat on the sofa, willing it to come soon.

Before it did, Mike came downstairs. Out of sight of anyone, he handed me a pile of pound coins.

'I didn't mean to do that Kat,' he said. 'I am so sorry.'

Back in my own bed, I couldn't get my head around what had happened. Why were people doing this to me? Was nowhere safe?

It became a new and horrible part of my week. The trip to that family members house. Being sent up to Mike's room (for my safety!). The assaults.

Like the other man, Mike didn't talk whilst things happened. He would force his hands between my legs and all I could hear was his heavy breath and the TV. As the months went on, he grew rougher. He would pull me onto the bed and force my head on his arm so that I couldn't move at all. Then he would press his body onto mine and make ghastly noises deep into my ear.

It was as if he had thought, 'I can do more – she isn't going to say anything.'

It didn't happen every Friday. Sometimes we really would just watch TV. Now and again, Dad would drop into the room, and they would casually chat. But whenever he got up to lock the bedroom door, then I knew what was coming.

One night I just couldn't take it. He had his hands down my pants and what he was doing with his fingers was so painful. I was in an armlock, so I couldn't move to free myself. But my head was on his arm. I turned – and bit deep into his skin. Blood went everywhere. On my to shirt, onto his arm.

He jumped off and I could see that he was angry. What might he do to me now?

'Taxi!'

The voice from below. 'The taxi will be here in two minutes.'

Mike told me to sit where I was and initially I did.

Meanwhile, he slipped on a jumper, to cover his arm, then went downstairs to fetch my coat.

By the time he returned, I was sitting on the floor, just rocking. I was in such shock. It was like I was trying to forget that anything in this room had taken place, ever.

'Put this on,' he said passing over my full-length coat. And then: 'Here. Take ten pounds.'

Back home, I hid the bloodstained t-shirt under my pillow. When I returned the next day from school, it had gone. Mum never mentioned it, and nor did I.

By the time a third family member tried to abuse me, I was alert to what was going on. I was able to save myself. I was able to shout out and prevent an attack. But how devastating that I should know already the ways of perverted men. Just a few weeks shy of my 13th birthday I had been subjected to revolting attacks that should never happen to anyone, let alone a child.

This family member had called the house and asked if I wanted to go to the park with a bunch of cousins. It sounded great fun! When I got in the car, though, it was just me.

'Oh, they're at the park already,' I was told.

He drove to a deserted stretch of land, that wasn't the play park at all. Then he stopped the car and locked the doors.

'If you ever needed anything, I would always pay you for sex,' he told me without preamble. 'I care about you. You're my number one,' he added, pulling out a small bottle of spirits, then drinking straight from the glass rim.

I watched in horror as he then put down the bottle, unzipped his trousers and reached inside.

Next, he leaned over to me and grabbed by hand, moving it towards his penis.

But I was ready! I pushed back my arm to free myself and began punching on my side window with both hands.

I was terrified. This family member worked in security and the place where he had stopped was a deserted site. It was pitch black outside.

'Let me out! Let me out!' I shouted, even though I wouldn't have known where I was, or been able to get to safety if I had been let out of the car.

And then the mood changed. Dark to light. Imminent attack to re-buttoned up trousers.

'Someone has done this to be you before, haven't they Kat?' he asked in a voice you would expect from someone who cared, not someone who had been about to abuse you.

'No,' I said firmly. 'Just take me home.'

He went to a McDonald's drive thru first. I put the Happy Meal he insisted I have on my lap. I had never felt less like a carefree child. I used the food box as protection on the journey home.

Several nights later, this man was back at my door.

'I need to know who hurt you,' he said. 'When I find out, I'm going to kill them.'

In recent years, there has been talk in our family that this family member was himself raped at age 13 by one of his brothers. Horrific as that is, I see that as no excuse. I have never wanted to carry out anything harmful to another person.

Despite, or because of, my adverse childhood experiences, I have always been determined to do good and to look for it in others.

6. WHY WON'T THEY BELIEVE ME?

Invisible within my family, abused by people I should have been able to trust, I turned to the church for help. But the pastor and his wife who I confided in let me down. By chance, there had been a young person in the congregation who had made (unfounded) sexual allegations about this pastor. So when I told them I was being abused, they panicked.

Whilst kind to me personally, they said that they couldn't get involved in case it would go on to be thought that perhaps the pastor had also abused me!

As my 13th birthday approached, however, I was beginning to snap. At a friend's house, her father looked at me sleazily.

'Now you are *really* good looking,' he said in a way that no man of 40 should say to a very young girl. Dad used to borrow money off this man and somehow, he had got my phone number. He sent me texts saying what he wanted to do to me, and how he would pay me for sex. I changed my number. He managed to get it again.

Wherever I went it felt that there was no escape. I couldn't handle the pressure. In my head, I had weighed up that putting up with the abuse (even by two men) was better than losing my family. But now that balance was tipping. When the third family member collared me at home, I accidentally let slip who one of my other attackers was.

Now I knew I had to act – before he did. To add to the pressure, a girl I was friendly with at church was saying if I didn't speak out, then she would.

That very Friday, I did the bravest thing of the my young life: I told the truth and kept telling it, regardless of the horrific reaction I got. A couple of days earlier, I had rung the family member whose house we went round to. 'Can we have the whole family over this week… ' I'd asked.

Granny who was disabled was unwell this evening, so she wasn't in the living room when I began. But my two attackers were present, as was mum, dad, my sisters, and several members of the wider family.

'This has been going on for six years,' I said to a room that had developed an icy silence. 'It needs to stop.'

Dad came to my rescue in that he took me out of the room. For something to do, we went to Tesco.

'I let you down,' Dad said. 'From now on, I will protect you.'

The following morning, the atmosphere had changed. When I went to hug Dad, he pulled away.

'I will support you about that boyfriend. But you must stay silent about the other person,' I was told.

Mum took it further.

'It's your fault,' she told me. 'You shouldn't have worn a vest top. Michael isn't the full shilling. If he did it, he was only playing.'

Several days later, Granny asked to see me. I told her how I had bitten Mike's arm.

'Give me a minute, I'll talk to him,' she said. When she returned, I could see that she had been crying.

'I do believe you, but Mike often comes here to help me,' she explained. 'If you speak up to the police, then he will be taken away.'

So my first abuser was right. My telling the truth would break up the family. It wouldn't just be about no one speaking to me; Granny, who I really loved, would suffer too.

In the end, the decision about whether to go to the police was taken away from me. My original abuser went to the police instead – and told them that I was a liar. He wanted me to be prosecuted for slander! Later, I discovered he had done this because his girlfriend had thrown him out.

'Prove your innocence by going to the police,' she had blasted.

At the police station, I was assigned a lovely support officer.

'I am so sorry this has happened to you,' she told me, and it was the first time anyone had ever thought about me and what I had been through, rather than their own feelings or discomfort. With her kindness and care, I poured out that there had been two attackers and that I had faced sexual abuse over six, desperate years.

'You poor love. You haven't had a childhood, have you?' she said and I could tell that she was holding back tears as well.

The interviews lasted long into the evening. It was, would you believe, my 13th birthday. What a day to commit to memory.

I arrived back home shattered. No charges were to be brought against me and instead what I said was to be investigated. But this was the early 2000s. There wasn't the overwhelming support for the victim that there is today.

Incredibly, for example, I was told that there was no point doing a medical examination, because just proving that I had ever had sex wouldn't be enough. I was 13. It was what some 13-year-olds did. My attackers were questioned, then later released without charge. My word was not going to be enough. When I returned home, I had it out with Mum.

'I told them about Michael,' I shouted.

'You're nothing but a liar,' she retorted, chasing me around the house. 'He went to a special school. He wouldn't have known what he was doing.'

'So that gave him the right to abuse me?' I said, as coldly as I could.

No reply came back.

For the rest of the family, life more or less carried on. it felt like a betrayal that they could still sit about and share meals and casual chat with this family member knowing what he had done to me. They still include him in get-togethers, but I keep away.

I drive past him most days on my way to work and it makes me angry that he can still walk the streets, despite what he did to me at a time when he was meant to protect me. It makes me angry, but I am not scared of him. I think that is because he did eventually say sorry and showed some remorse.

The other relative threw out her boyfriend. For a few years it looked like she may not have done. She's not with him now, but I do know where he is, which continues to frighten me. Just about the last thing that he said to me, face to face, was on the night when I exposed him.

'I'll get you for this,' he said. 'You won't get away with it.'

He is an evil man. I remain terrified of him.

7. HANDLING THE FALLOUT

I f I thought I was invisible beforehand (to everyone but my attackers), in the weeks and months following my speaking out I truly disappeared. As someone whose whole ethos was about being good and pleasing others, having to deal with being the cause of upset was hugely unpleasant.

There were days when I really did wish the abuse was still going on, just so that I could enjoy what closeness I'd had with Mum and Dad once more. I couldn't bear how I was now thought of as a liar. My head of year at school was kind.

'If I could, I would adopt you,' she would beam. 'You are a truly lovely and kind girl.

When it got even worse, I thought about death as an end.

'No one cares,' I told myself. 'There is no point to my life.'

Mum and Dad both took medication, which was kept in a box by the sink. An overdose would be easy for me to organise. Could I go through with it?

In total despair, I rang Childline. We had been given Childline key fobs at school, and I had kept mine safe at home, just in case. On that day, the wonderful, caring person who answered my call saved my young life.

'You are the bravest girl I have ever spoken to,' I was told. 'I spend a good deal of my time on the phone talking to boys and girls whose mum and dad have just shouted at them, and of course it's important that they have someone to listen to them. But you! I am in awe of how you have been through so many terrible things, yet you have survived. Now, take your time. Tell me just how it feels…'

Her real interest in me and what I had been though encouraged me to pour out my unhappiness and despair. An hour passed. I heard Mum and Dad arrive home and I could tell that they were drunk. I told the Childline counsellor that I would need to go.

'Call back when you want. We are always here for you,' she said.

I didn't call back because just that one call was enough to move me on from wanting to end my life, to understanding that I *could* cope with what I had been through. It would be difficult, but it wasn't impossible

Seven years later, I trained as a Childline counsellor myself. I needed to give something back. Plus, I knew that I would be able to emphasise with children going through truly tough times. I did it for a year and remain proud that I was able to do this.

The summer after I had spoken out, I went on a church camp. When I came back, one of my distant cousins who is older than me needed to speak with me urgently. It turned out… the boyfriend had tried to do to her what he did to me. It was many years ago and she said that she would tell if he ever tried to touch her again. He didn't, and so she hadn't said anything. But then a family member had told her mum about me and her mum had told her and she'd spoken up.

'He tried to do that – I'll kill him,' had been my Dad's response.

It was the same again when a third girl said he had come on to her some years ago when she was around 10.

Suddenly, because it happened to other girls too, maybe I was to be believed as well. No one called either of these girls a liar, and people wanted justice for them. It was so unfair! I felt confused, let down – and very angry.

Disappointingly, the police said that each case had to be looked at separately. Which meant there was still insufficient evidence. No charges were made. At home, it became a non-conversation. It was as if the abuse and my revelation of it had both never happened. For my part, I blocked it too: I wouldn't read books or watch TV programme that might feature abuse. I never spoke on these topics with friends.

I have never been attracted to men, and I wonder if what happened to me had some part in that. When I was 14, I had a boyfriend who was 16. We held hands and kissed, but I didn't feel anything. Then when I was 16 I met a woman who was also ready for a loving sexual relationship. It was lovely and I was relieved to find that what happened to me as a child didn't get in the way.

Straight after the abuse ended, I used school work to distract me. No one in our family had put much into education: my middle sister truanted from around age 12 and our home wasn't exactly full of books!

When I was 16, my oldest sister told me about the Rape Crisis centre. There was this random street in Belfast and you had to find a blue door and knock. There was no sign, and this was for everyone's safety. The support I received from here was phenomenal. People gave me the space to talk, and then listened without judgement. Some years later, I began to train as a counsellor. But it was too traumatic for me, and I had to stop.

Around this time, I was also subject to a vicious attack on a day trip to the city. Two friends and I had been having fun taking pictures in a photo booth when some other girls came over and started butting in. I told them to leave, and they did. But later, as my friend swore because she bumped into a metal bar on the booth, these girls attacked us. They pretended we had been swearing at them.

First, I was grabbed by the hair, then a pint of beer was poured over me. I was so angry that I lunged at a security guard, who then escorted us outside. Then the fight really kicked off. There was a hostile crowd of 13, against just us three. One girl swung her fist at me, whilst a guy with steel-toe boots kicked me on the back of my knee. I didn't stand a chance. My head smashed onto a marble floor, where I pretty much stayed until the police arrived.

I have a bald spot to this day where my hair was pulled. But I am grateful not to have been seriously injured. In court, the girl who had punched me pleaded guilty. She was already out on license, so was returned to prison. She was 23 to my 16.

It won't surprise anyone reading this story that I was eager to leave home and my home area just as soon as I could. But it took violence to make me do it.

One night, when Mum and Dad were arguing I intervened. I grabbed at Dad and he fell and banged his head against a wall.

'You think you are such a big girl,' he said and smacked me.

I phoned for the police who came very swiftly.

'Did he hit you?' I was asked.

'Yes.'

A cousin confirmed that he had witnessed this too.

'I don't want you to take him away. I just want to scare him,' I said, and it was true. Based on my wishes, the police decided to simply record the incident in their notes. But if there were to be a next time…

Shortly after that night, I moved out. I went to live with another cousin who had a place close to the college I had joined after GCSEs. It was time to discover who I really was. I felt free to be me – but a little nervous as well.

8. IT HAPPENS AGAIN

I had two relationships before I met Amy. One was a lovely 'early' relationship that gave me a hint of what it might be like to be in a couple where each person valued the other. She had my name tattooed on her body, but then she moved away with her family and things faded away. We knew however that we would always be friends.

My second relationship lasted around a year. It ended suddenly and a little acrimoniously when she went off with a mutual friend. In hindsight, the best bit was the bond I had formed with her mum. She came to love me like a child and this continued long after I stopped seeing her daughter.

Then came Amy, who I've written a little about in the opening chapter. She told me that my family were horrible and didn't care about me, but that she did.

Our early honeymoon period of cosy TV suppers or party nights with pals ended abruptly one Saturday evening.

'I feel like slapping you,' she said as we watched *The X Factor.*

'Nah, don't be silly,' I said, then noticed that two friends who had come over for the evening had gone strangely quiet. Whack. Amy's hand walloped my cheek.

'What the —'

I was too shocked to say more.

'Huh. Just felt like it,' said Amy. 'All done now.'

It seems bizarre to me now that we all carried on just as we were. But we did. For some reason, it felt important not to show Amy that I was crying.

But 10 minutes or so later, I couldn't keep it in. I began to sob.

'Why you crying Kat?'

'Because you hit me.'

'No. Not me. Girls!' she called across to our friends, 'Did I hit Kat?'

I missed the warning sign that neither of our friends said anything. They couldn't stand up to Amy either.

Over the following weeks, the disarming process of casual violence, then denial of that violence, was repeated time and again. There was a third element too.

Later, she would be extra loving. She would buy me flowers. She would tell me I was beautiful. But then would come another day, another situation, and her mood would zig-zag again. She didn't work, so it was my money that paid for bills and food. The puzzle now is what on earth I got out of that relationship.

Once she spat on me, full on the face and just because she could. I became so stressed that I returned to the rocking motion I had first used on Michael's bedroom floor all those years ago, after I had bitten his arm.

One of her 'make up gestures' was to buy me a dog (she had one already). Pretty soon it became clear that the dog was a new way that she could get at me. Instead of hitting me, she would hit my dog. It was a sure way to ensure I did whatever she wanted – buy more beers, clean the house – because I couldn't bear the dog being hit (whereas it was 'OK' if I was).

There were few limits to her cruelty or coercive control. She wouldn't let me look at my phone, but read my messages. She knew about the child abuse, yet she forced me to watch brutal rape scenes. 'I'm rewinding this, so we can see it again,' she would taunt.

Only in bed was she kind.

'I really love you Kat,' she would say. 'Don't ever leave me.'

Once, she threw an iron at me. Fortunately it landed above my head and the wallpaper, not me, got burnt.

Outrageously, it is my (unproven) belief that she faked a kidnapping of herself in order to get money and my full loving attention.

One day, I took a call from 'kidnappers' demanding a ransom. Within hours, the police had found her, tied and bound at a remote spot. It made the TV news, but no one was caught. The net result was that I left work. If this could happen – she denied it had been staged – then I needed to be at home. It was what she wanted: me at her beck and call, 24/7.

I don't believe she was even faithful to me. She would go out partying, or hold parties downstairs to which I wasn't invited.

On one dreadful day, I hit her back. She had been smacking me and laughing in my face all night. I lost my temper and smacked her with such force her head went flying into the sink.

'Got you now,' she said. 'If you ever leave, I can tell the police that you hit me. In fact, I may just tell everyone that you are an abuser.'

My moment of temper caused me to stay a few more months. I found work in a burger bar. I bought her things. I did my best to do exactly what she wanted. Then one night she said that I was rude about her in front of her friends.

'I love you Kat. But if this were to happen again… well I need to show you what would happen to you,' she explained. Then, we got into her car and she drove at break-neck speed down a very long hill. She slammed on the brakes at the bottom just in time.

'Next time, I won't stop.'

It's the final and frightening straw. Amy was mad as well as cruel. The next day, I took the dog to Mum's, for safety.

'What should I do Mum?' I said.

'Stay if you love her,' I was told. 'Stay and have a life like mine. But if you want something more, then walk away.'

I spent a week or so planning how to leave.

'You're so fucking ugly Kat,' she told me a few nights later. 'No one but me would want you.'

I waited until she had gone out for the evening before I threw a bag of clothes together. I had decided to leave the pictures on the wall and the plates in the cupboard that were mine. I wanted no reminders of my time here.

I removed my social media profiles. I blocked her and all our friends from my phone. I was 20 years old. If I wasn't brave now, I knew I would be dead or sectioned into a mental institution within the year. I hadn't been through the most horrible of childhoods to be floored now. I took courage in both hands and slipped into the darkness.

9. THE ROLLER COASTER YEARS

When Amy's friends threated to 'get me' and burn down my home, there was only one place to run: to the amazing mum of my-ex girlfriend. She took me in when I turned up and put her warm, safe arms around me. As well as the fact that Amy knew where my own family lived, I didn't want to face more 'I told you so's' from my parents and sisters.

Eventually, I found a place to rent a few miles away. I could afford the bills easily enough because I now had a job in a care home and, with little else in my life, I was always up for overtime.

I liked how I could focus on the people I cared for, yet they wouldn't ask anything about me, or my back story.

In time, I met another woman. Again, she appeared good-natured and interested in me, but neither turned out to be especially true. Like Dad, her mood dropped when she was 'in drink.' She took party drugs too (something I have never been into). Most of our home and leisure time was about her, doing what she liked to do. Again, I was paying more of the bills and receiving less of the love.

In 2016, I heard about The Truth Project. A UK government initiative, its ambitious aim was to gather the testimony of thousands of victims of childhood sexual abuse. It is hoped that these statements – 'The Truth' – will lead to far better handling of victims by the police, criminal justice departments and social and health care clinicians.

I am proud to be one among 6,000 victims who came forward to be interviewed in Liverpool, where the project was based. But taking part wasn't without emotional cost.

'That was rape,' the investigator told me, no punches spared, once I told her my very shocking story.

Yes, of course it was, you the reader may be thinking. But I had never applied that word to what had happened to me. I knew that it had been abuse, of course. But rape?

I wonder now if not being able to use that word was part of denying the full atrocity of what happened, in order that I could keep on handling my being attacked week after month after year.

When I returned from giving my statement, I went into meltdown. I went on prolonged sick leave at work. Much of the trauma that I had squashed down so that I could get on with my young life now flooded out. I had PTSD big time.

One night, I decided I had had enough. I had a car by this time and decided that I would get into it and drive to a local lake, then keep on driving into the water. I remember getting into the car and the absurdity of doing up my seat belt in those circumstances. I did and didn't want to end my life, so I texted all the friends I could think of, with the hope that someone would call me right back and stop me.

But no calls came in.

Finally, just as I pulled into the lake, I managed to come up with a compelling reason to live. My beautiful young niece Becca. She was about eight years old then. What trauma would I be putting her through if she had to deal with the fact that an aunty had killed herself?

There was nothing I didn't know about childhood trauma and how it can take the best part of a life time to shake off. Did I truly want to be the cause of that trauma in another child?

I switched off the engine and sat in my car and wept until I had no tears left. Now that I was going to live, I had to find a way to make it bearable. I knew I couldn't do it alone. I drove home and resolved to seek professional help.

Over many months, I saw a wise, kind lady. Finally, I came to forgive myself for what had happened, and to accept I was in no way to blame for what these men did to me. I was not responsible either for my parents and how they behaved towards me.

I saw all this and started to want better for myself. My partner at the time, however, was not able or willing to give me the support I now came to recognise I deserved. Although we were technically still together for a while longer, in my head I switched off.

I have taught myself techniques to regain calm. When repulsive images from my past flash up, I begin to drown them with music. Today, I keep headphones nearby and the delicious positivity of Christina Aguilera singing *Beautiful* or *The Climb* by Miley Cyrus work wonders. I also like *Fight Song* by Rachel Platten. It reminds me that I am OK being exactly who I am and that when there's a rough patch, I can fight on.

As if everything I had been through as a child and young adult wasn't enough, by the time I moved into my mid-20s, my physical health began to decline. I had suffered with endometriosis for some years. This then progressed to a severe form of bowel disease that needed major surgery.

The operations went well, but the care home where I worked was not sympathetic. I had been studying at home and was at a point where I was ready to begin at university, with the care home company as my sponsor. They had suggested this path for me, but now they withdrew that option.

My response was to leave. I secured a job within a prison quite by chance, and quickly found it was absolutely for me. I was in a caring role as a health assistant and, as ever, I found it easy to bring kindness and empathy to my work.

It also sparked a further academic interest. I began a degree in criminology. I realised that I had an ardent curiosity about *why* people became abusers, murderers and rapists.

Studying criminology awoke a dream to one day work within the justice system. If I go on to have a job interview in that field, I can imagine myself saying, 'I want to see people punished for the crimes that they do.'

That's hardly surprising considering what I have been through – and how no one has been punished for what they did to me.

It might sound contradictory, but it is possible to be empathetic towards criminals, yet also want punishment. The key for me is that punishment is fair and just. Once that has been done, everyone is entitled to live a free life.

10. LIGHT AND LOVE AT THE END OF THE TUNNEL

I met my amazing fiancée at work. I was drawn to her from the start, but because she was seeing someone else I kept well away. So much so that one day she said to me, 'Whenever I walk into a room, you walk out. Why is this?'

As well as being aware that she was seeing someone else, I walked out because I had believed she would never take a second look at me. She was - and is - beautiful, strong and courageous. By now too, I had had so many bad relationships and so much trauma that I guess I was scared to begin another relationship.

Then, one night at work, when I was upset at how my previous partner behaved, she told me I didn't deserve to be treated like that. It was the first time I had ever received such words of comfort... and I fell for her.

When we were both free, we began seeing each other. It was, and is, magic. After our first date at a restaurant, she rang me within 10 minutes.

'I need to see you again now,' she said.

'What's wrong?' I asked.

'I have just shared the most amazing kiss of my life,' she said. 'I need another one fast!'

We became engaged last year and have set a wedding date and venue for 2025. At last, I am with someone who truly loves me, just as I do them. There is a calm and consistency about the life that we share and it is this which I relish so much. I don't want drama! What I *do* want is being able to say what I feel and never to quake in fear again at how someone will react to me simply being 'me'.

My university degree is going well and I continue to enjoy my job. Mentally, there are still both good and bad days. The difference perhaps is that I now accept this. I also have a safety net in place: it consists of my partner (clearly), a brilliant GP and a counselling service that I am able to call up anytime. Sometimes, a few texts with the counsellor is sufficient. Or I might need a series of therapy sessions. It would be wrong and unhelpful for me to suggest to anyone reading this who has suffered abuse that you can ever 100 per cent recover. But the level of 'OK' I am at now feels fine.

Always, though, new shocks can leap out of the woodwork.

For example, only last year I discovered that the family member who abused me in his bedroom had admitted what he had done to some people in my family *more than a decade ago.*

But no one thought to tell me.

So I lived all those extra years needlessly thinking everyone believed I was a liar. A travesty. Today, people continue to invite him to their parties, even though they know that means I will miss out. Where is the kindness and decency in that?

My fiancée says that I should go along too, and that she will be there, right beside me. Who knows. Maybe one day.

Putting my own needs first is still something I find difficult. For example, even though my parents could have done a great deal more for me through my childhood, I don't stint on helping them, now that they are older. I do shopping for Mum. I give generous gifts. Dad is 60, mum is 63, and the kind of lifestyle they have led is catching up with them health-wise.

I don't forgive my abusers. They each knew what they were doing and it was over a sustained period. But I have forgiven my family, including my sisters and cousins and uncles and aunts who didn't step in or notice how troubled I had become. It's harder to forgive my parents, but hand on heart, I do. What I refuse to do anymore, however, is only say what might please them. I get that parts of this book may be a tough read for Mum and Dad in particular. So be it. Trying to please everyone has back-fired on me time and again.

I'm on the fence about whether to have children myself. My fiancée and I talk about it - no decision yet made! But if I were to become a parent, I would ensure just about everything was different from my own childhood.

At the start of this book, I said that there is always light at the end of the darkest tunnel, and my story is proof of that. But life isn't a train journey. You can't take a seat and sit back waiting to reach the light. You have to be brave, and push yourself to be able to recover. And you have to keep on being brave.

Let me reassure you that it is always worth it! Now that I am personally happy and professionally satisfied, my life is totally worth living. The dreadful things that I suffered have made me into the woman I am today, but finally, I like that woman. I am happy to be who I am.

Whilst I hope my story may inspire others, I have written it in no small part for myself. I make no apologies for that. Victims of abuse are invisible. I needed to be able to put down in words that:

This was real.

This happened to me.

This is my truth.

Everything that I have written, I take full and personal responsibility for. Any errors are accidental memory lapses or are the result of subtle changes, designed to preserve the anonymity of everyone concerned.

Once, I had a horrible life. Now, I see a future that brims with purpose, meaning and joy. Whatever your situation, I wish you well.

SUPPORT & ADVICE

I f you have been affected by any of the issues raised in this book, these organisations can offer advice and support.

Childline is a free service, provided by the NSPCC, which supports children and young people under 19. Childline counsellors can take calls 24 hours a day, 7 days a week. They are also available to speak to online through 1-2-1 chat and via email.
Visit www.childline.org.uk
Call 0800 1111

Samaritans is a registered charity aimed at providing support for anyone who's struggling to cope, who needs someone to listen without judgement or pressure.
Visit www.samaritans.org
Call 116 123

www.ingramcontent.com/pod-product-compliance
Lightning Source LLC
Chambersburg PA
CBHW072052040426
42447CB00012BB/3096